CONCUSSIONS

A Football Player's Worst Nightmare

Biology 6th Grade

Children's Diseases Books

BABY PROFESSOR

EDUCATION KIDS

We live in a high-impact world! You can bang your head on a door in your house, and it's even more likely if you play a contact sport. A bang can cause a concussion. Read on to get smart about concussions and what to do about them!

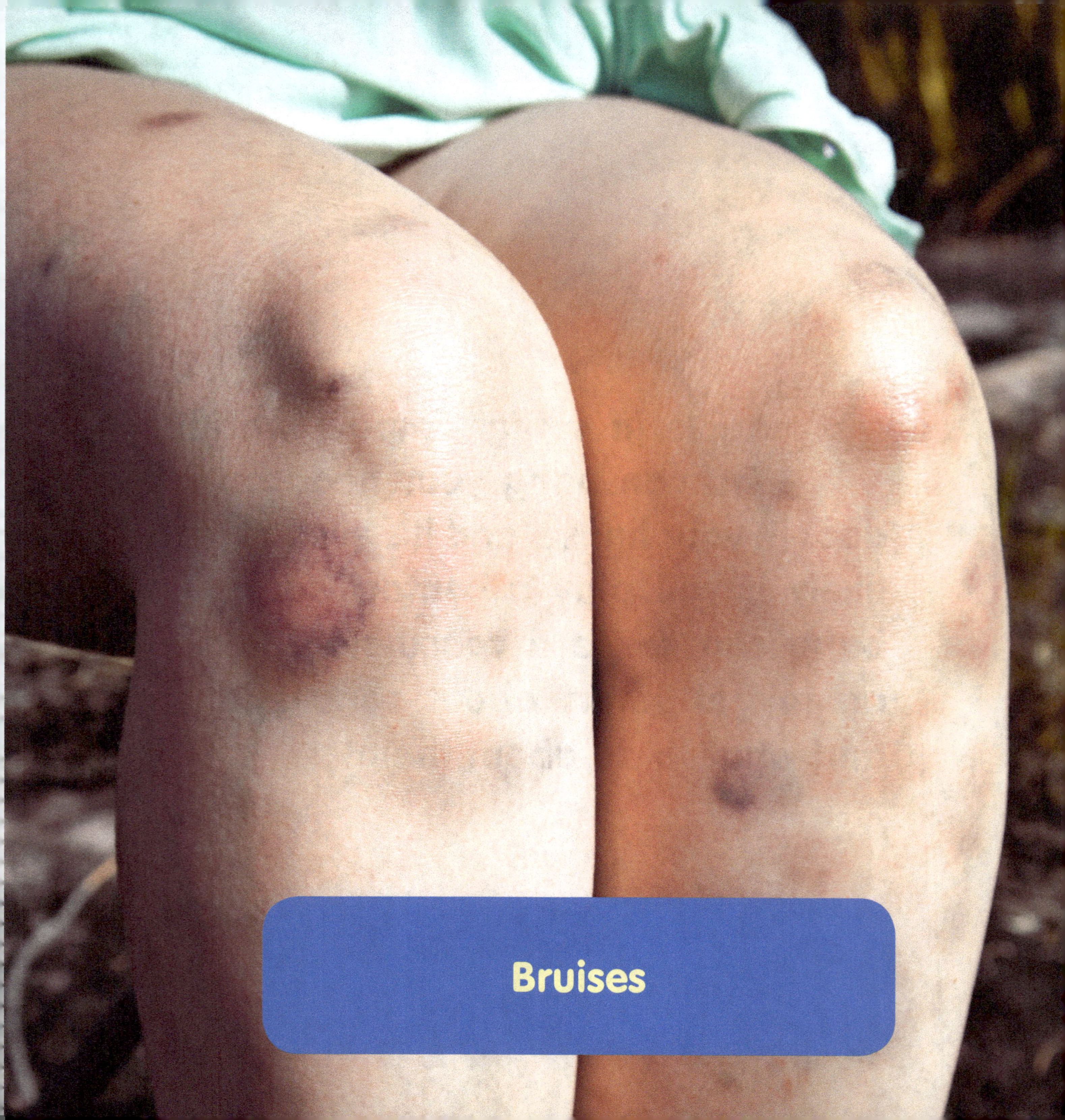

Bruises

MORE THAN JUST A BUMP

When you run and play, you sometimes bang into things. Your body is pretty tough, and most of the time you might just scrape your knee or get a lovely bruise that hurts a bit and turns all sorts of colors.

But the reason it hurts is that your body is warning you that you are doing something that may cause serious problems. When you stub your toe or cut your finger, your body is saying, "Be more careful! You need that toe and that finger!"

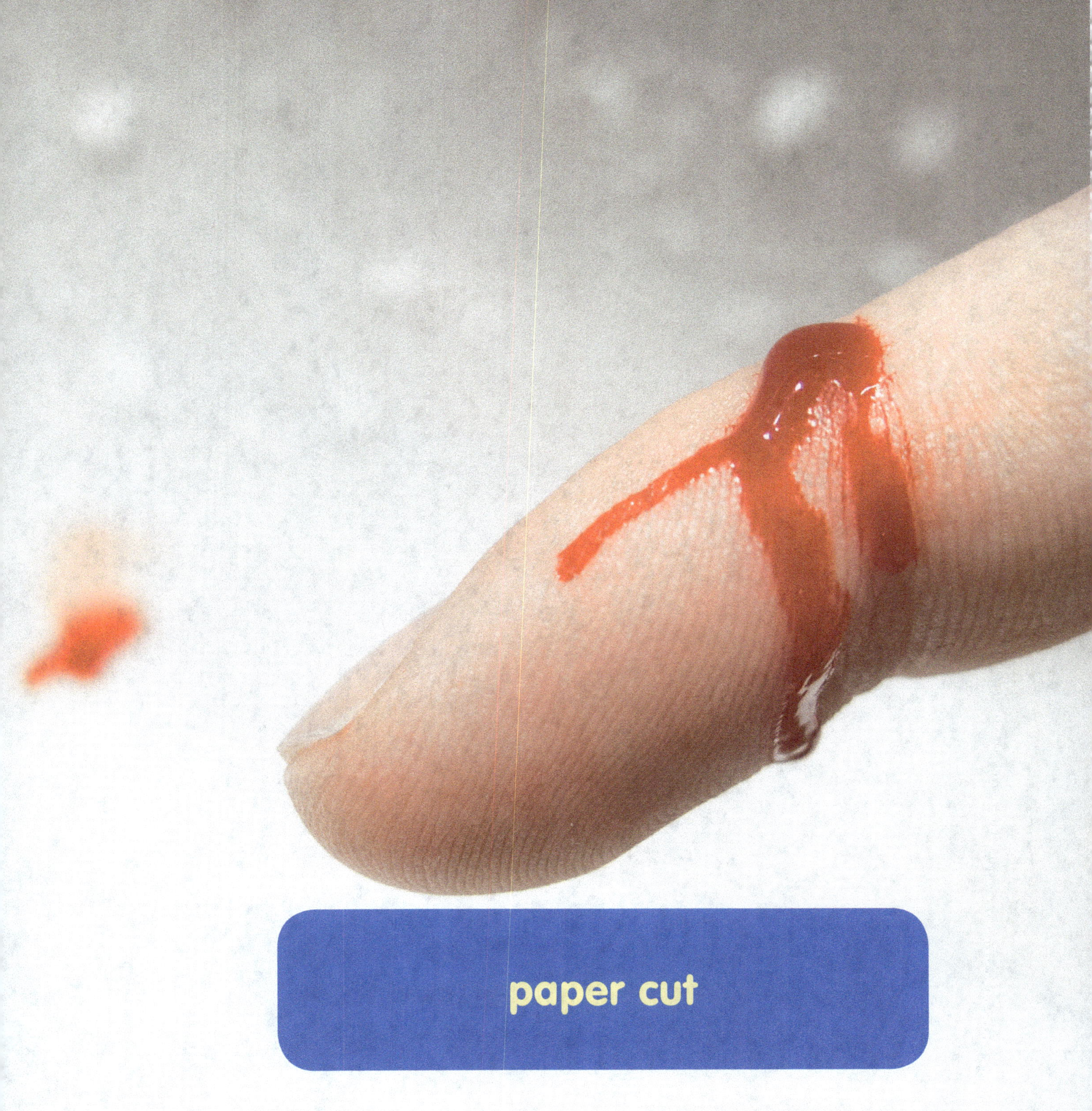
paper cut

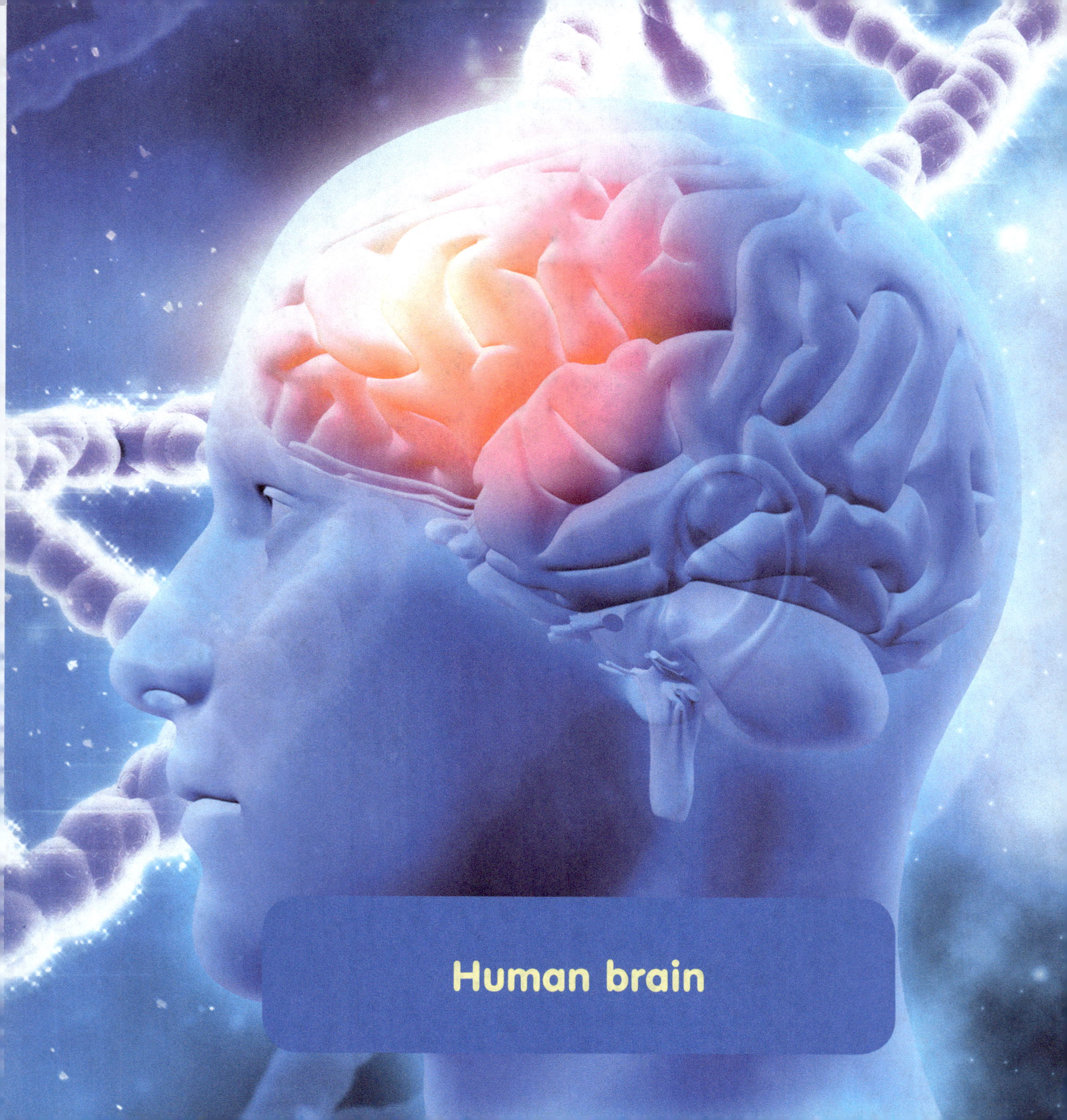

Human brain

All the parts of your body are important, but your brain is the most important of all. The body protects it well, but you need to help protect it, too. Because if something damages your brain, it can be a serious problem.

YOUR BODY PROTECTS YOUR BRAIN

Your brain is inside your skull, which is like a helmet under your hair and scalp. If you knock on your head with your knuckles, the skull feels pretty solid.

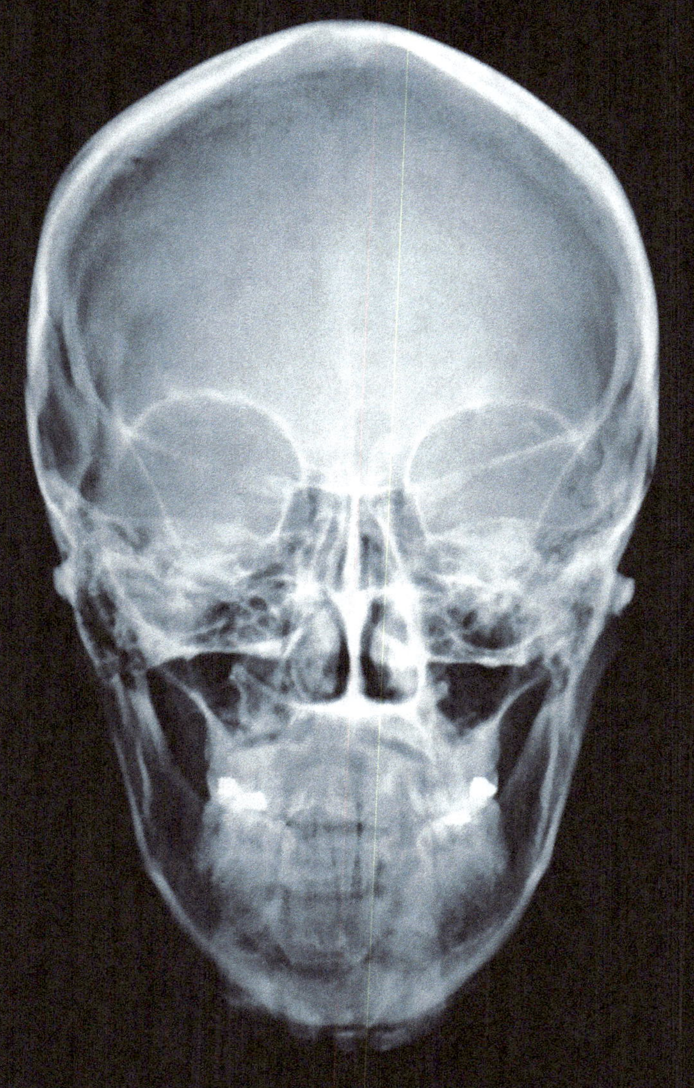

Skull

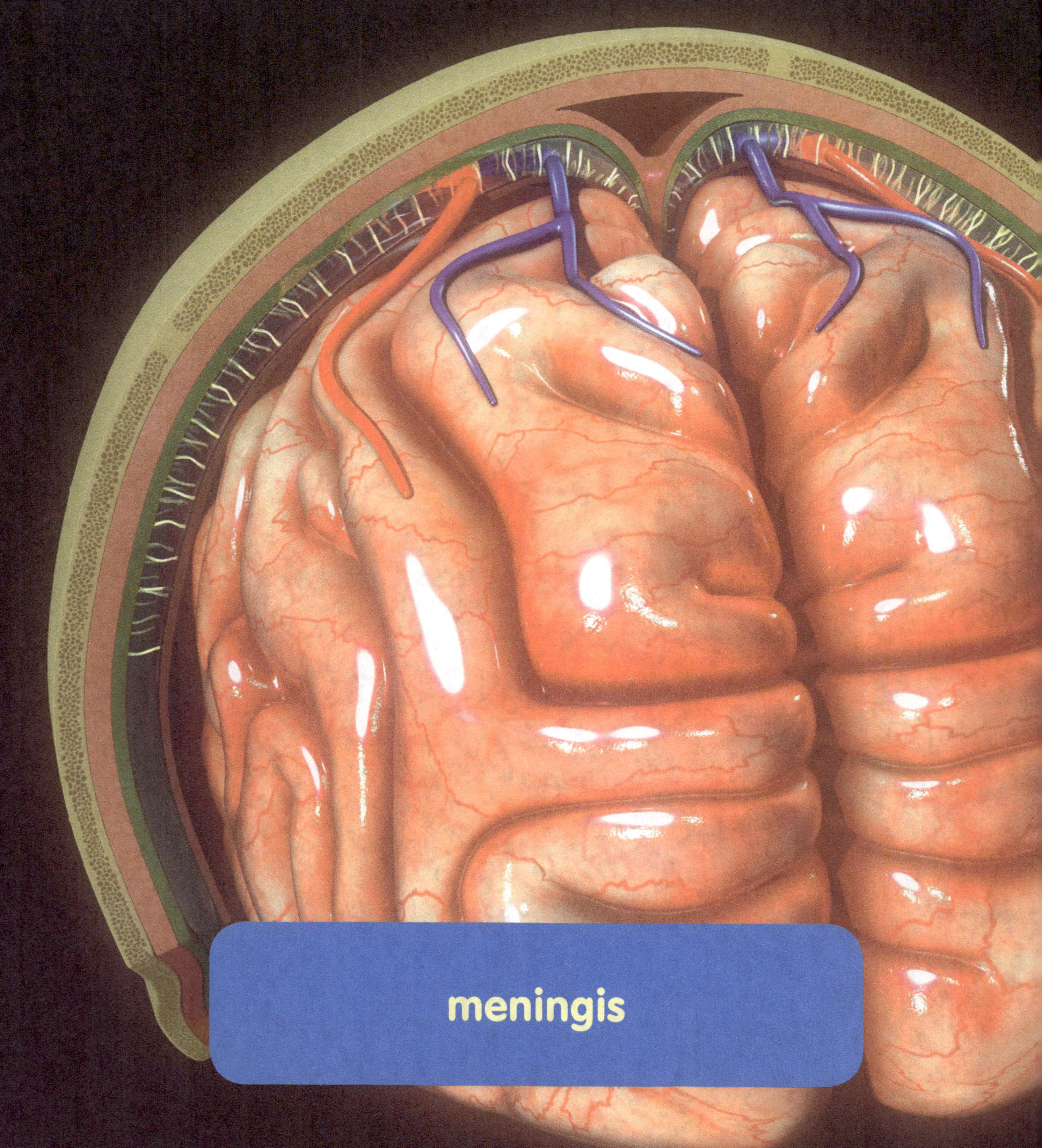

meningis

Between the inside of the skull and your brain are membranes called "meninges" and a layer of fluid. They are there to cushion the brain, and when minor bumps happen the brain just moves a bit in that liquid, which absorbs the impact. However, not all bumps are minor.

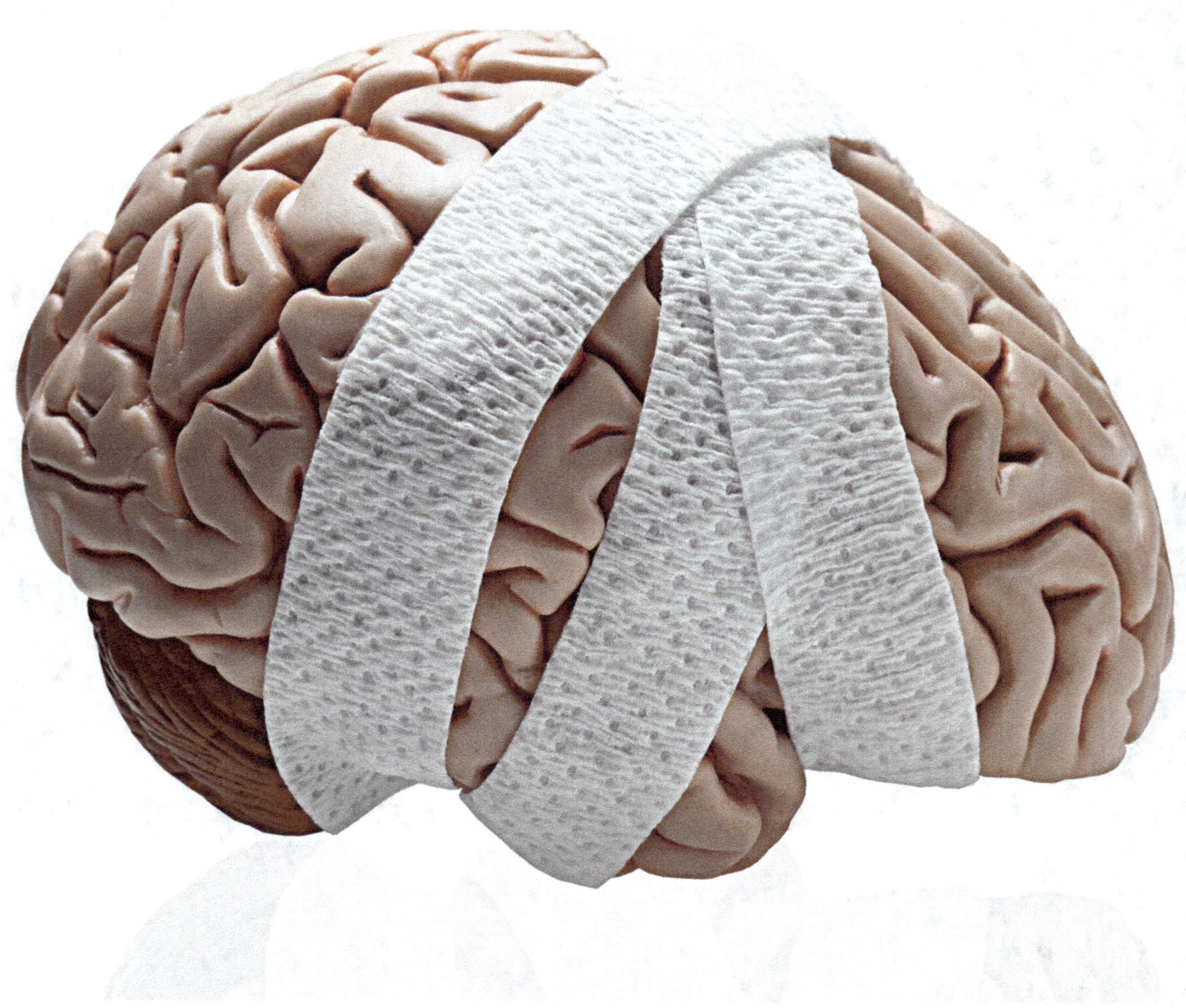

Injured brain

WHAT'S A CONCUSSION?

When you have a major bump to the head, your brain can move suddenly through its protective fluid and bang up against the inside of your skull. That collision can cause temporary or long-term damage to the brain.

If the bump is hard enough, it can change the way your brain works. And if that happens, you have had a concussion.

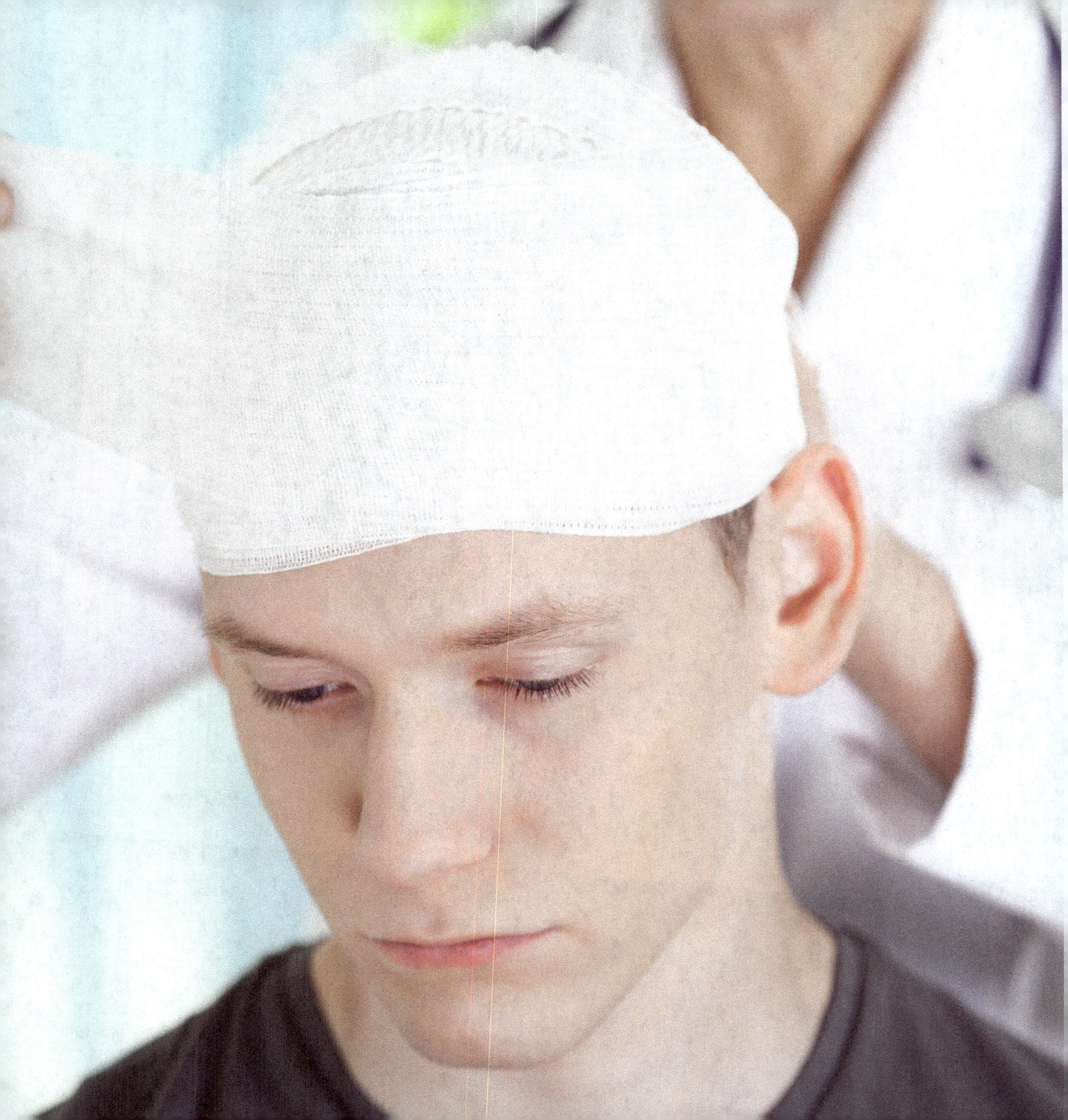

SIGNS OF A CONCUSSION

Lots of times it's not clear if you have had a concussion, even if you had a serious knock to the head. Your parents or the coach of your sports team probably aren't doctors, and in any case they don't have the right medical equipment to check you out while you're lying on the sidelines after a hard tackle in football.

I**f you have had a hard hit in a game, or have fallen off your bike and whacked your head, there are signs to look for. If you have any of these symptoms, get your folks or your coach to take you to a hospital right away. This is not something that can wait for your next check-up!**

THE SIGNS INCLUDE:

- You get knocked out, or you lose consciousness even for a few seconds

- You have a bad headache, and especially if it keeps getting worse

- Your vision is blurry

- You can't walk straight, or you get dizzy when you try to stand up

- You can't find the right words when you try to talk, or the words make sense to you but not to the people you're talking to

- You can find and say the right words, but they sound sort of blurred and unclear

- People have trouble waking you up, or getting you to respond when they talk to you or touch you

There are some other signs that show you have had a whack, but don't necessarily point to a concussion. If you have these signs, your parents should call your doctor and ask if they should take you to the hospital for an exam.

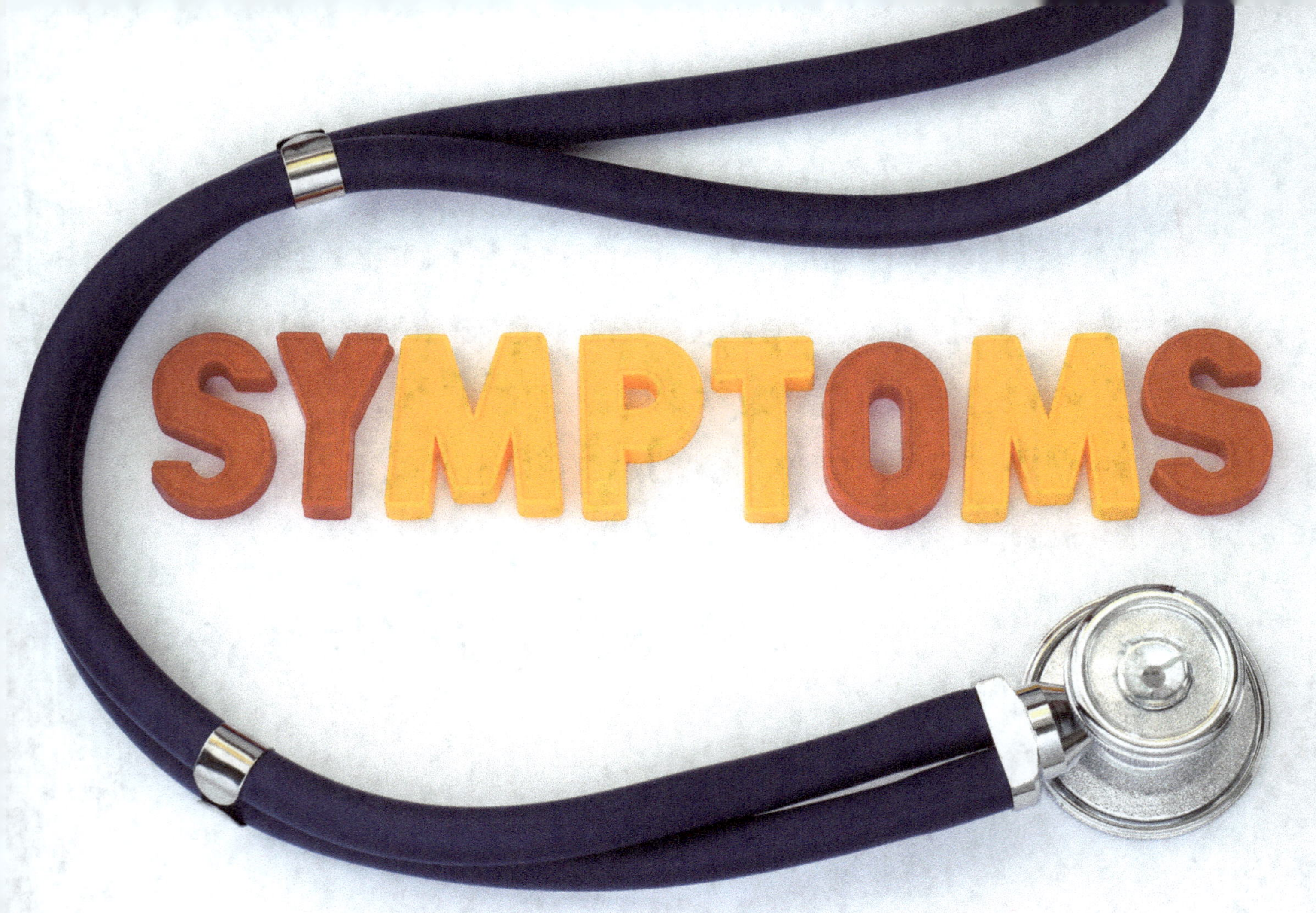

SYMPTOMS

These symptoms could show up even hours after your bike accident or when you got tackled during the game:

- Vomiting
- Dizziness even when you're sitting or lying down
- Headache that won't go away
- Trouble concentrating, reading, or even watching TV

WHAT HAPPENS IN A CONCUSSION?

Let's say you are playing a contact sport (not chess!) and you and another player bang into each other. By accident, his knee meets your head, with both the head and the knee moving very quickly. Bang! The other player probably hops around holding his knee, and you are probably down on the ground, seeing stars.

During the collision, your brain got moving too fast for the fluid and the meninges to absorb the impact when your brain banged up against the inside of

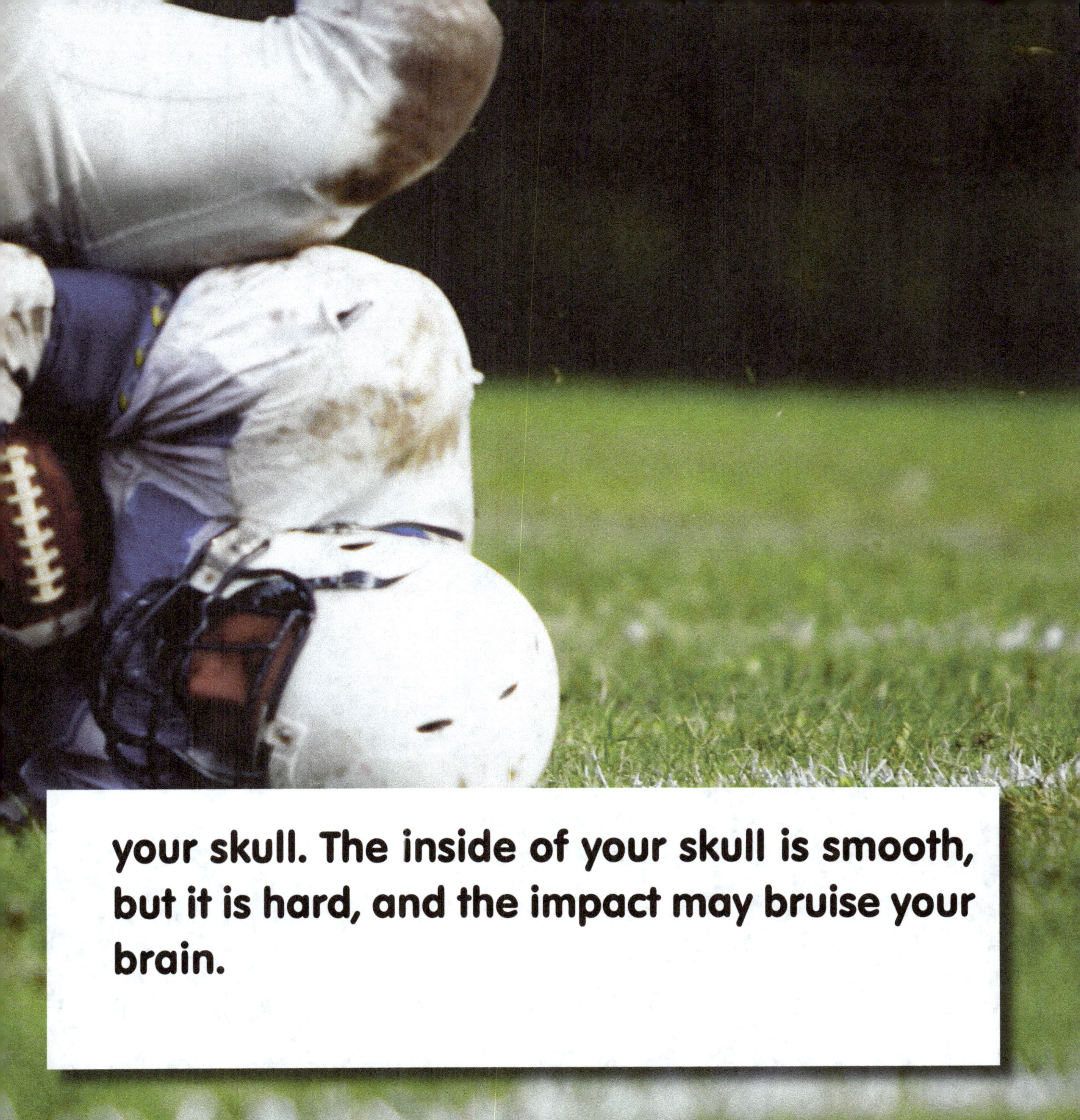

your skull. The inside of your skull is smooth, but it is hard, and the impact may bruise your brain.

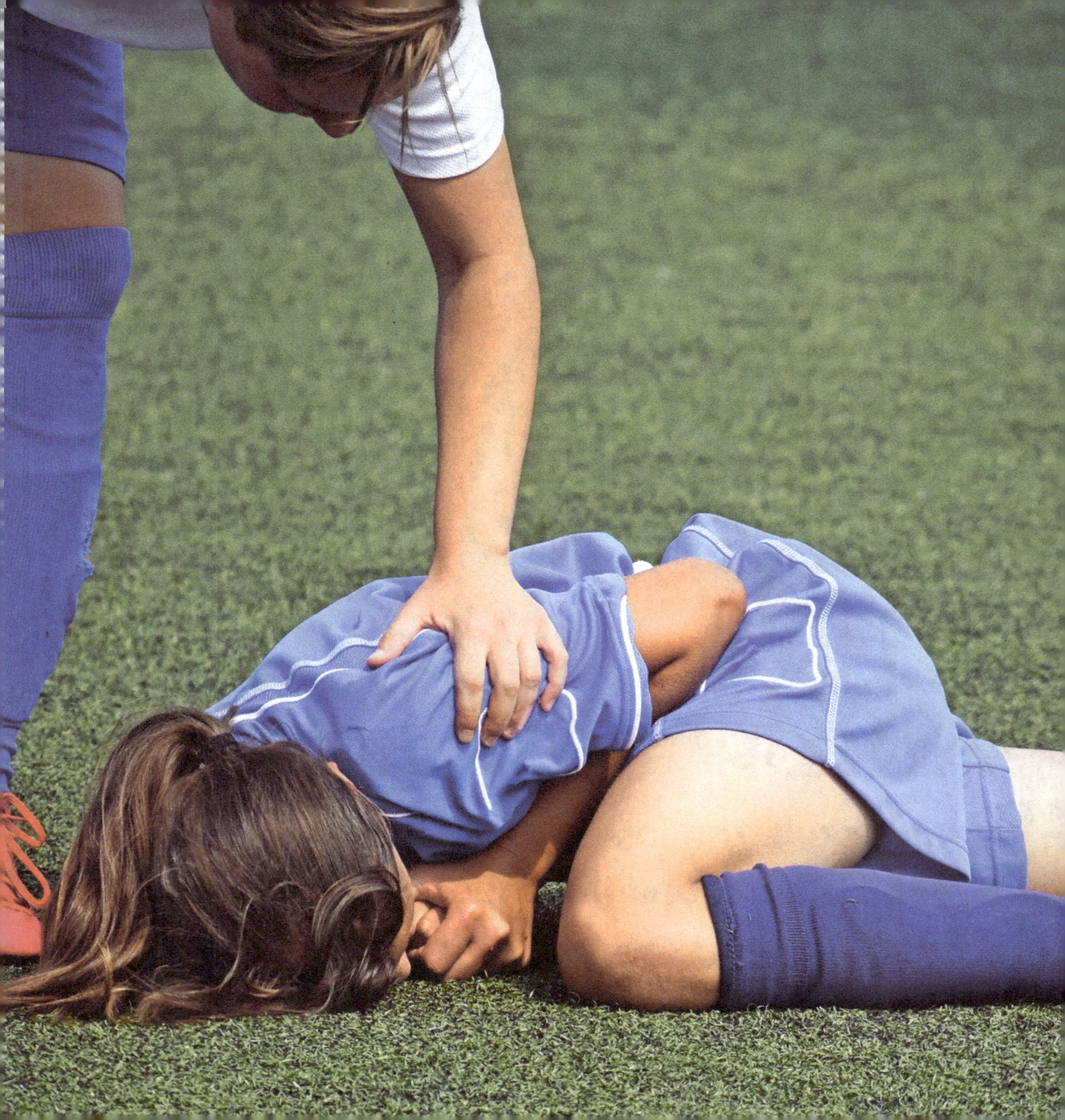

Also, different parts of your brain can move at different speeds when you and the other player bang into each other, and you can actually stretch or sprain the connections between different parts of your brain.

A third effect is that the balance of chemicals and ions in your brain and its surrounding fluid gets mixed up. It's not really like shaking a soft drink can and then opening it, but the effect is sort of similar.

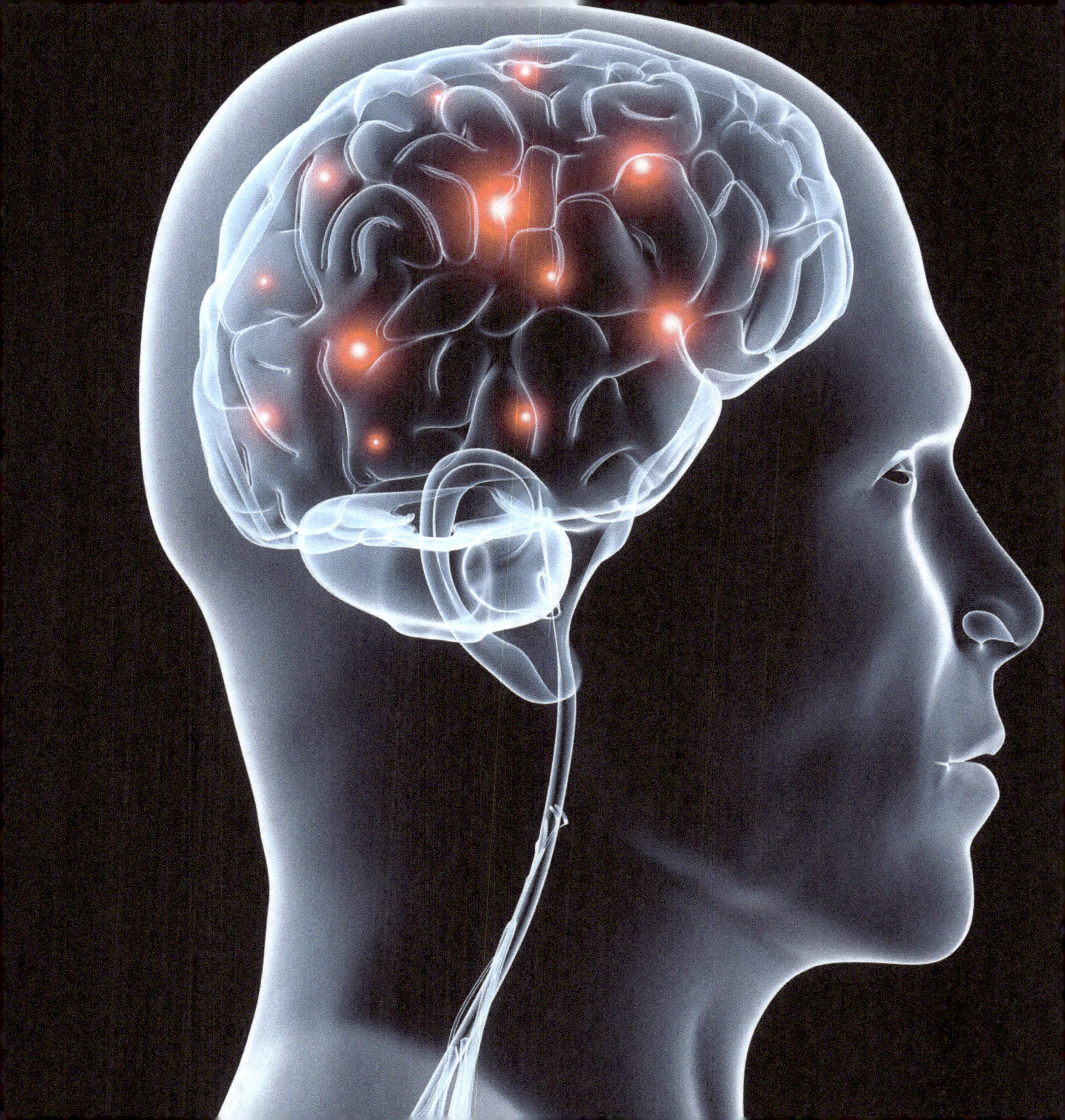

The wrong chemicals start trying to do the wrong jobs, slowing down how your brain can think and react to what your body is reporting to it. This is often why a person who hits their head loses consciousness: the brain has a bit of an overload and cannot respond well.

AFTER A CONCUSSION

The brain is very good at repairing itself, and the chemical and ion balance come back to normal pretty quickly. But there can be damage that is so severe that the brain cannot repair it. This can result in a permanent reduction in what your brain can do.

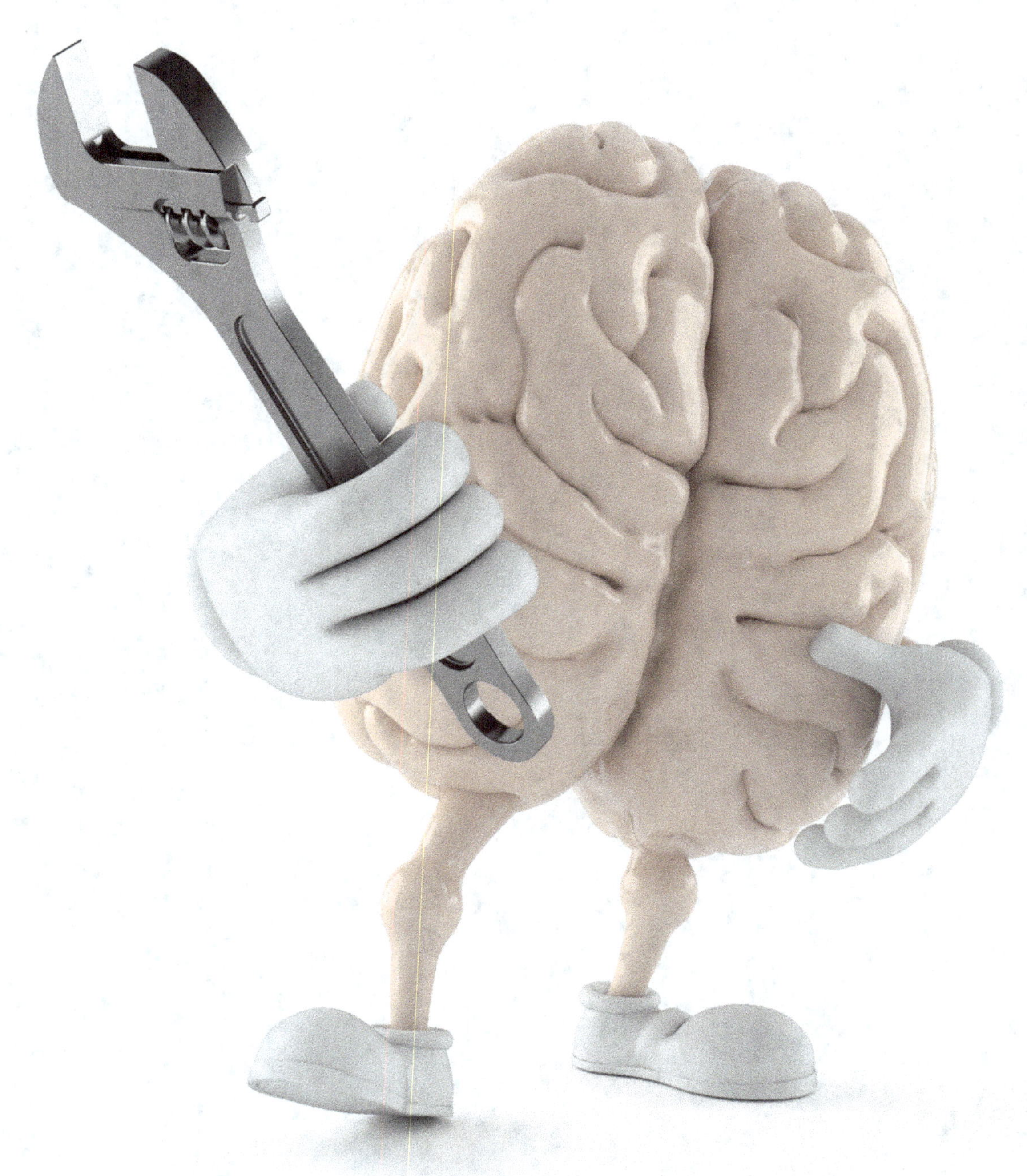

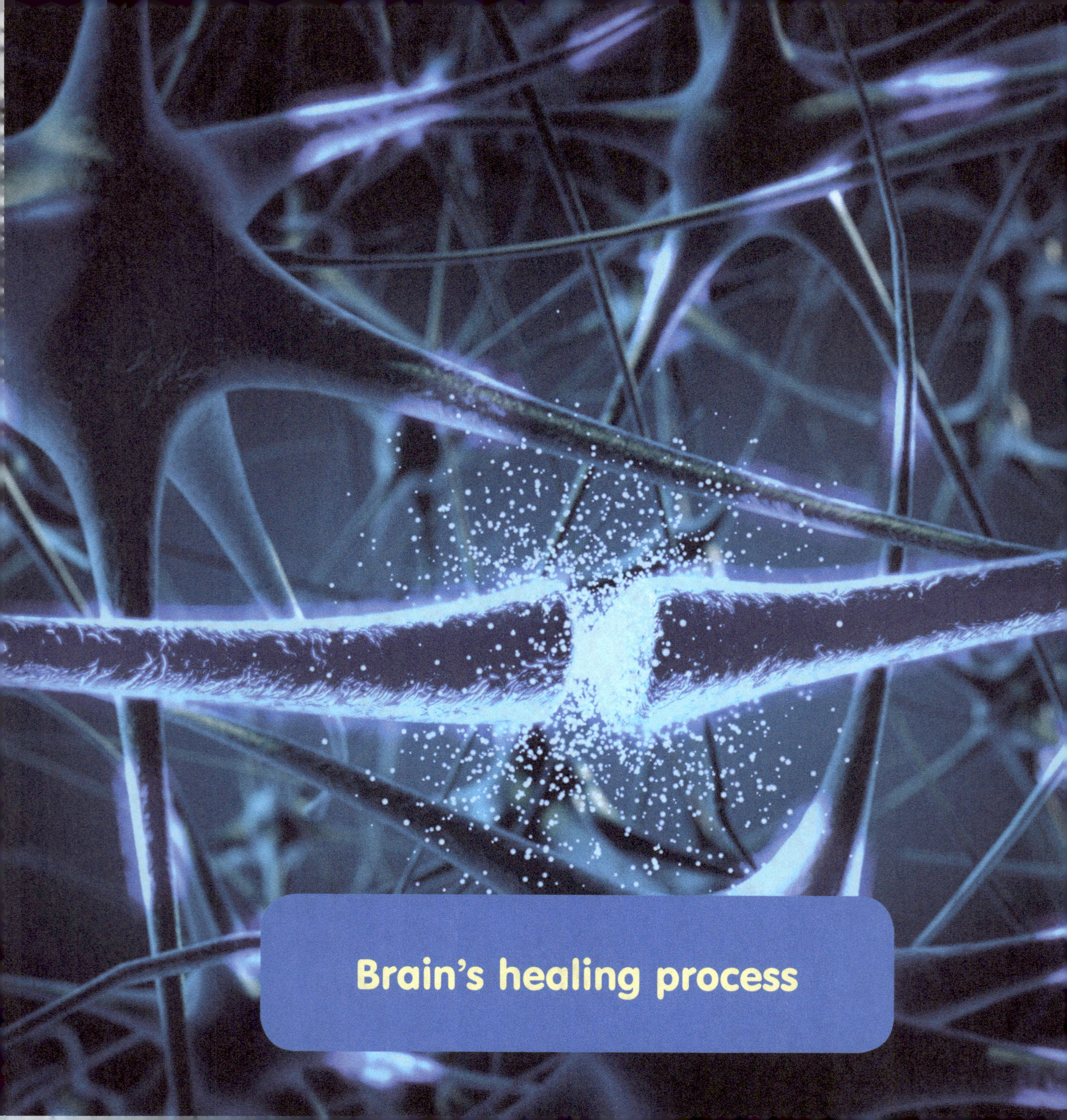
Brain's healing process

An additional problem is that the brain's confusion can cause some processes to start that the brain would not normally do. Your brain may start producing "free radicals", chemicals that get in the way of the healing process and slow down delivery of oxygen and nutrients to the injured part of the brain.

If there was a lot of bruising, the brain may swell in that area. That swelling may cause pressure on the rest of the brain, causing problems for functions that normally take place far away from the area of your brain where you banged your head.

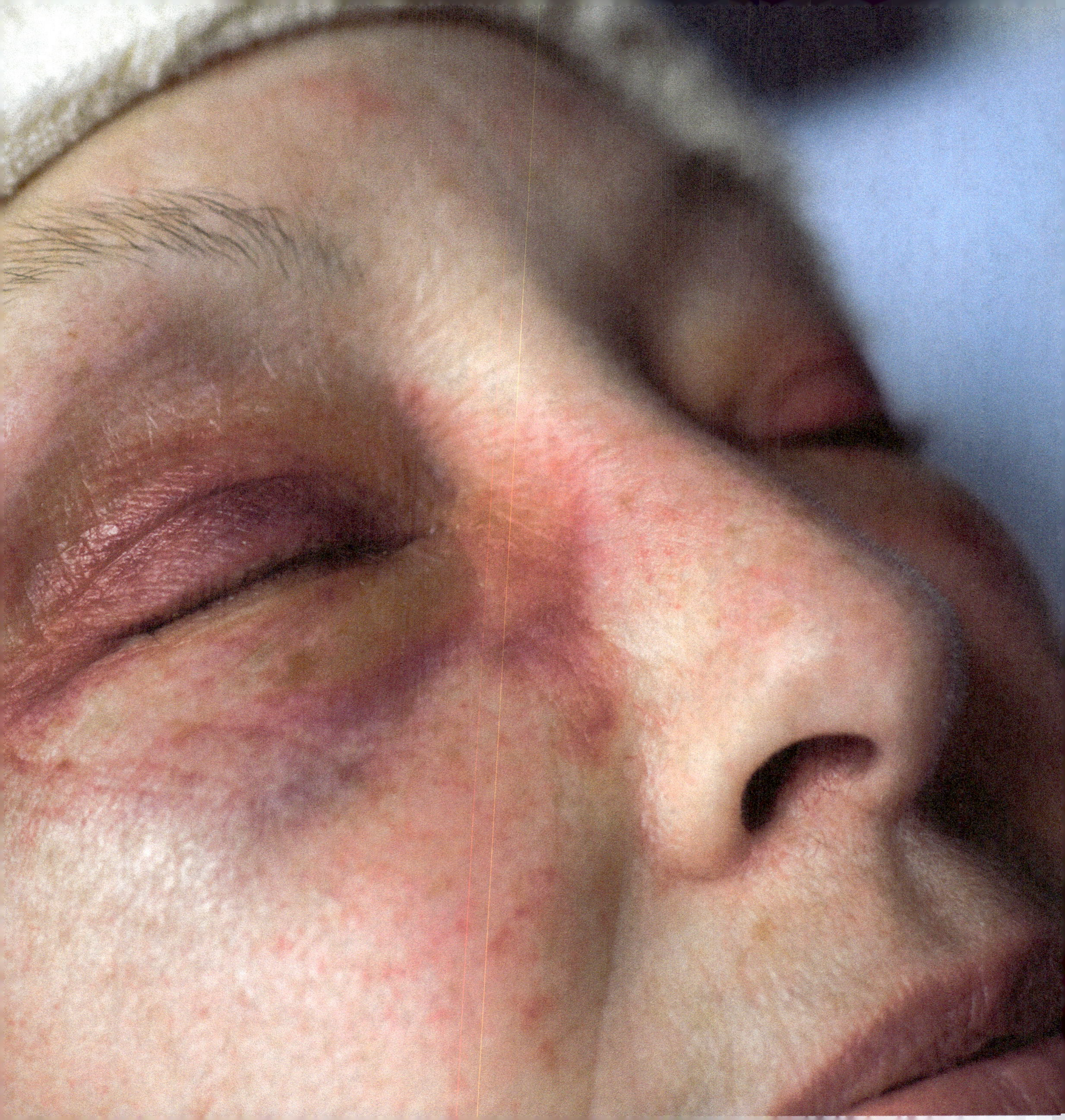

For some people, there can be fatigue, dizziness, trouble concentrating, nausea, and blurry vision for weeks after the collision, while the brain repairs itself. If the damage is serious, doctors have medicines and techniques that can speed the healing.

The worst thing to do after you have had a concussion is to pretend that you haven't had one. We've all seen heroes in movies who get blown up, beaten up, or involved in car crashes, and then in the next scene they're all perky and ready for the next adventure. Remember that that's in a movie. It's make-believe. The real world does not work that way when you get hurt.

Your best plan is to follow what the doctor tells you to do. That will probably involve a lot of rest and staying away from situations where you might hit your head again. There may be medicines or other treatments to reduce any swelling or bruising the brain experienced, or to help bring the chemicals in your brain back into balance. Listen carefully to what the doctor says, make sure you have the instructions written down, and ask about anything you don't understand.

Your worst plan would be to pretend to be a movie super-hero and go right back to doing what you were doing before. If you suffer a concussion in this week's game and try to play again before your brain is fully healed, what happens if your head meets another knee at speed? You may suffer an injury on top of the existing injury, and that might lead to permanent damage to your brain. You might lose the ability to see, or to walk, and you don't want that!

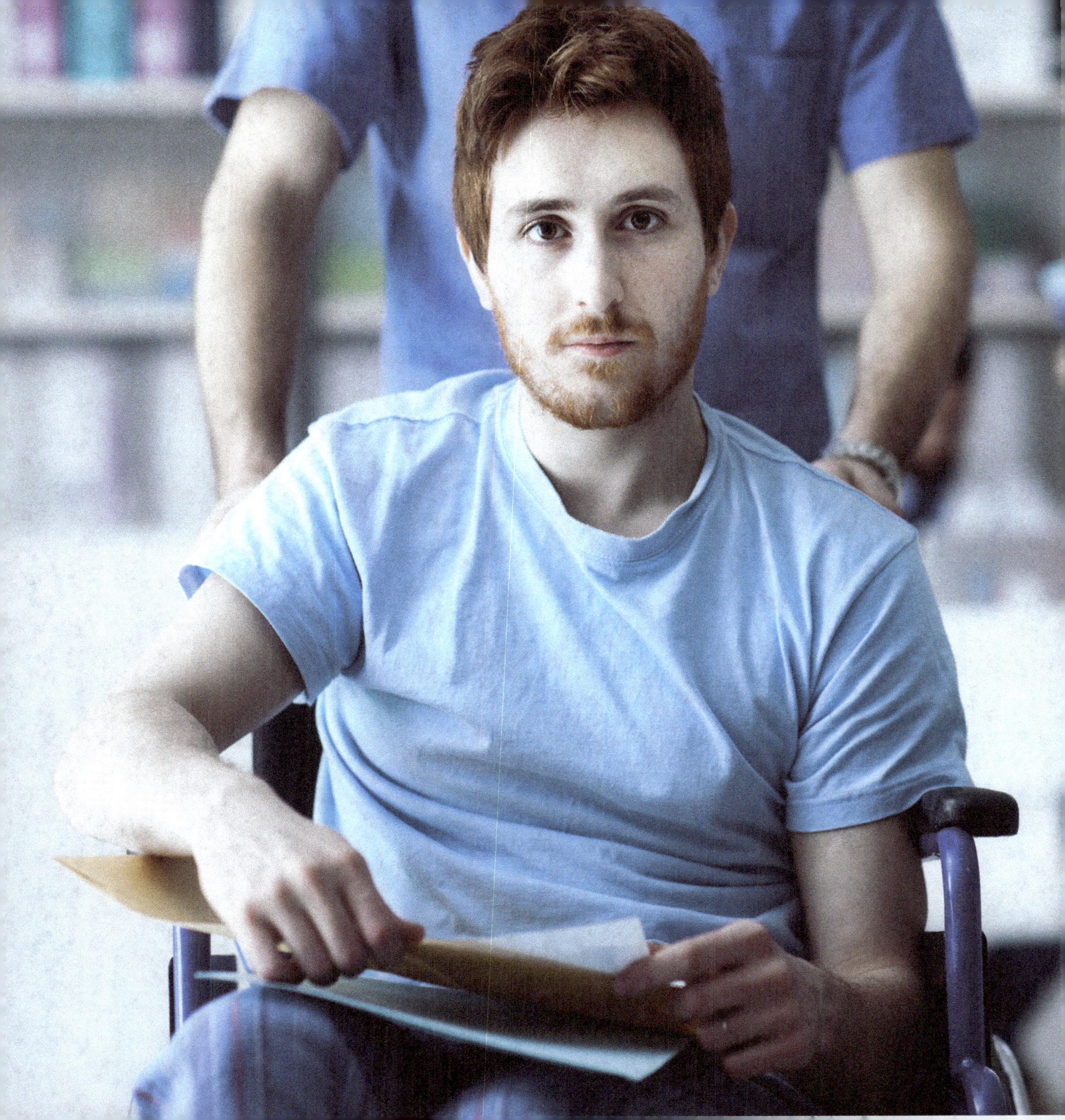

HELP YOUR BODY PROTECT YOUR BRAIN

You don't know when an accident is going to come and find you, so you have to prepare for sudden shocks. Here are some simple steps:

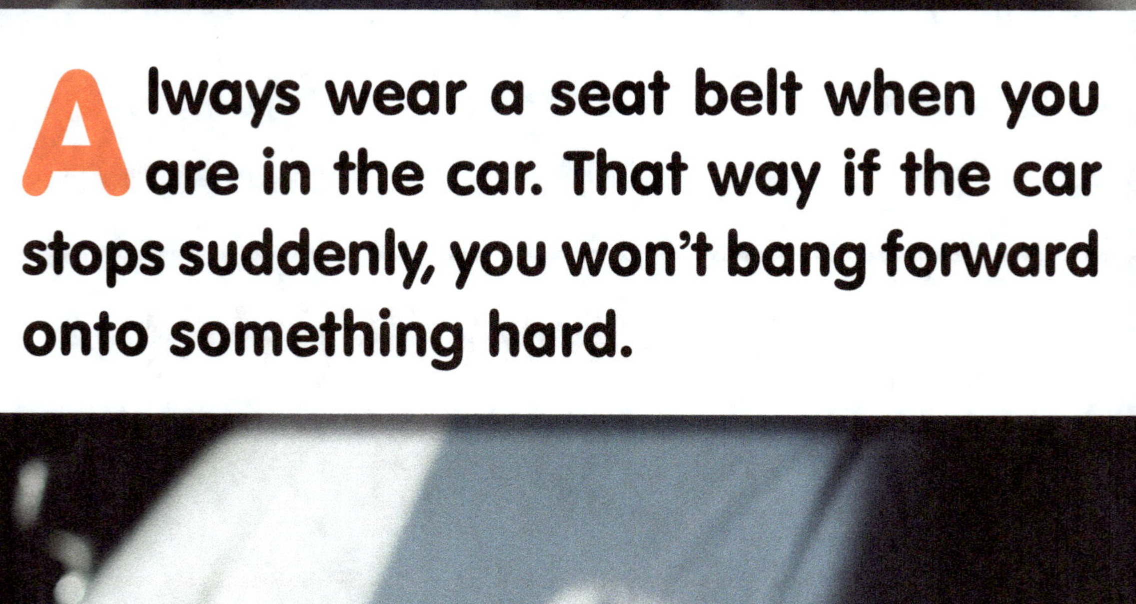

Always wear a seat belt when you are in the car. That way if the car stops suddenly, you won't bang forward onto something hard.

Wear a helmet when you're on your bike or skateboard. You may think it doesn't look cool. Well, people with permanent brain damage look, and feel, even less cool. A helmet won't absolutely prevent concussions, but it can reduce the effect of a fall. Don't be a super-hero. Tell the truth when you get an injury and don't try to play through it.

Wear all the protective gear they recommend for your sport. It's not worth the risk of long-term injury just to look more stylish or daring. Major-league baseball players earn millions of dollars and are the best of everyone who plays that game, and they are smart enough to put on their batting helmets before they get anywhere near home plate. Be as smart as they are!

Visit
BABY PROFESSOR
EDUCATION KIDS
www.BabyProfessorBooks.com
to download Free Baby Professor eBooks
and view our catalog of new and exciting
Children's Books